ESSENTIAL ELEMENTS®

GUITAR ENSEMBLES

JAZZ BALLADS

CONTENTS

Arrangements by Chip Henderson

ISBN 978-1-4234-6365-8

HAL•LEONARD®
CORPORATION

7777 W. BLUEMOUND RD. P.O. BOX 13819 MILWAUKEE, WI 53213

Visit Hal Leonard Online at
www.halleonard.com

BODY AND SOUL

Words by Edward Heyman, Robert Sour and Frank Eyton
Music by John Green

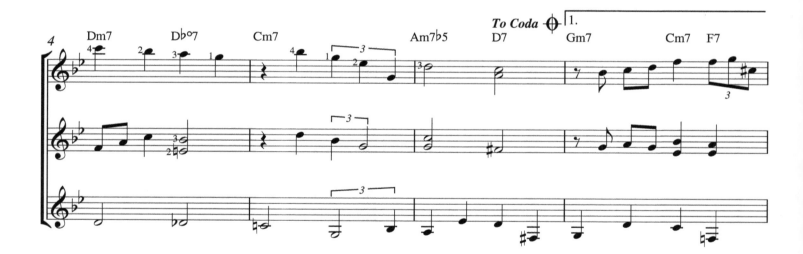

BUT BEAUTIFUL

from ROAD TO RIO

Words by Johnny Burke
Music by Jimmy Van Heusen

D.S. al Coda

Coda

A CHILD IS BORN

By Thad Jones

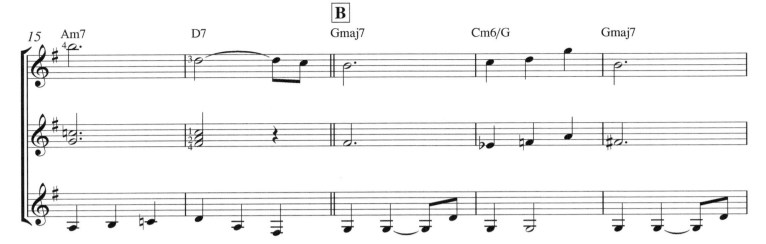

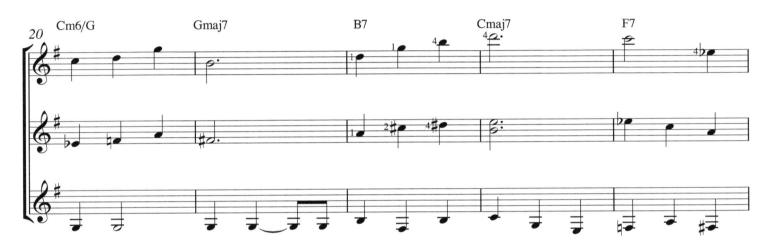

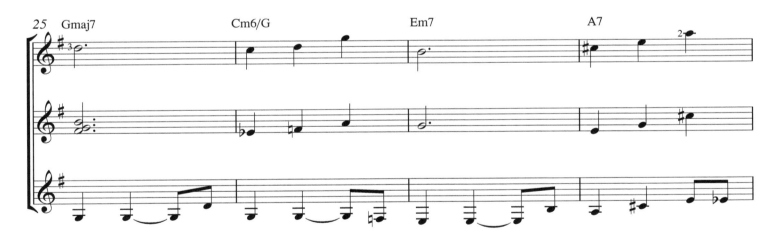

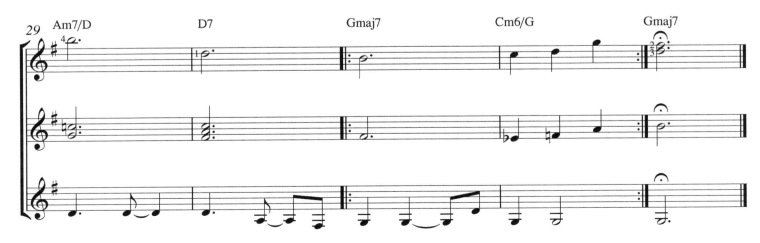

EASY LIVING
Theme from the Paramount Picture EASY LIVING
Words and Music by Leo Robin and Ralph Rainger

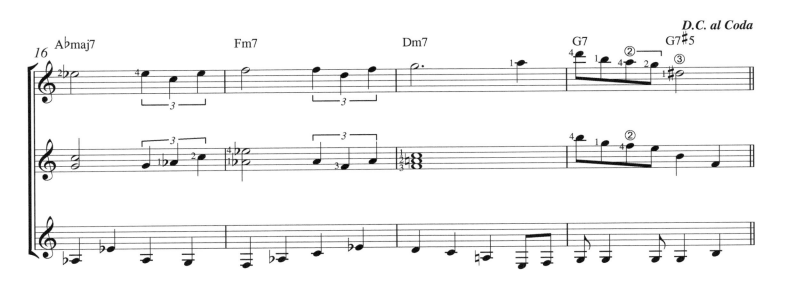

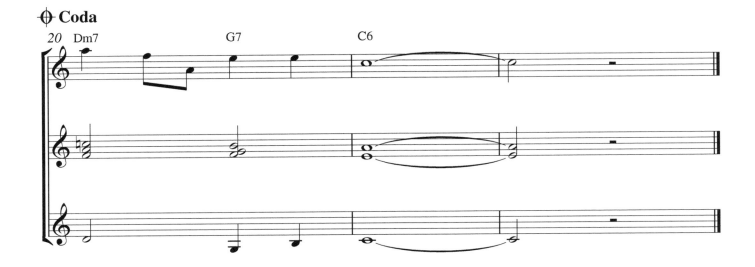

HERE'S THAT RAINY DAY

from CARNIVAL IN FLANDERS

Words by Johnny Burke
Music by Jimmy Van Heusen

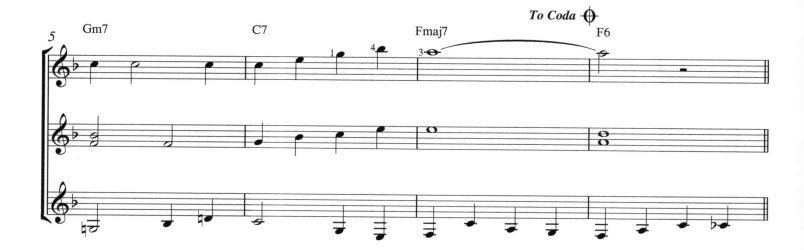

D.C. al Coda

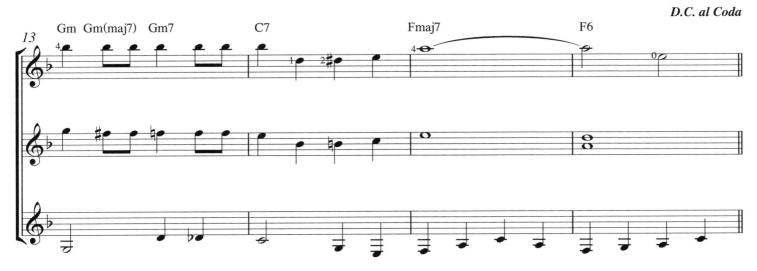

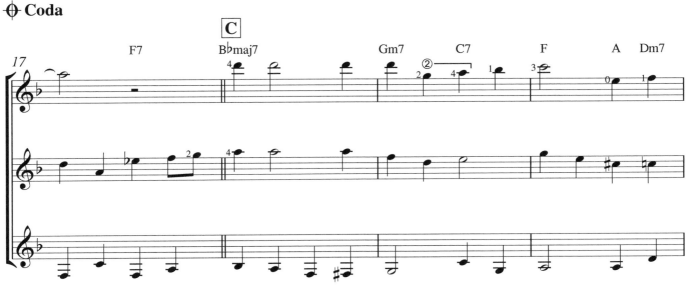

MISTY

Music by Erroll Garner

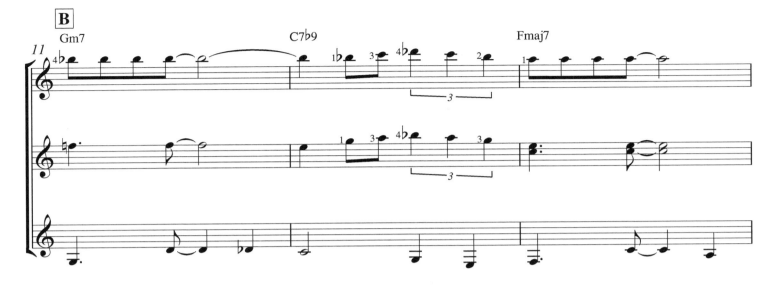

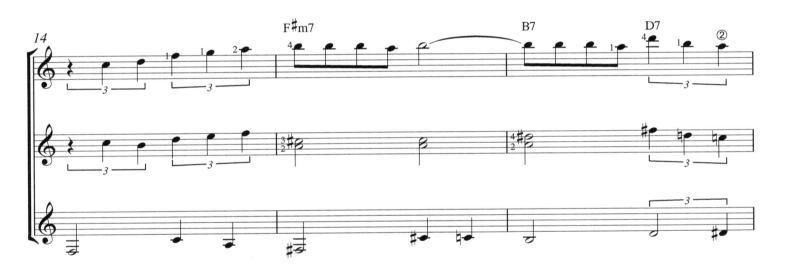

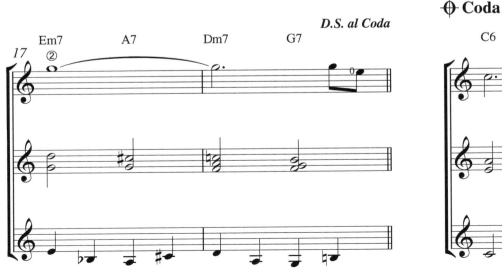

MOONLIGHT IN VERMONT

Words by John Blackburn
Music by Karl Suessdorf

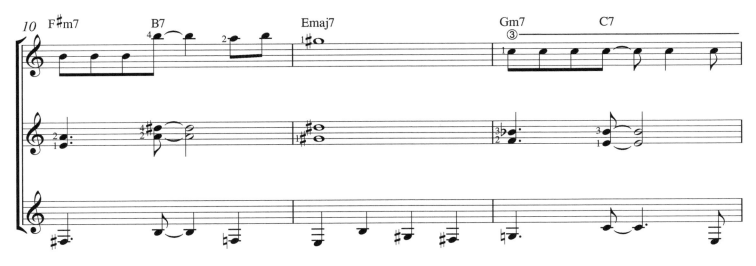

D.C. al Coda

⊕ Coda

MY FOOLISH HEART

from MY FOOLISH HEART

Words by Ned Washington
Music by Victor Young

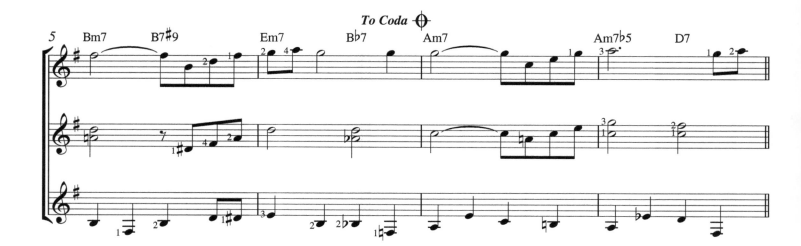

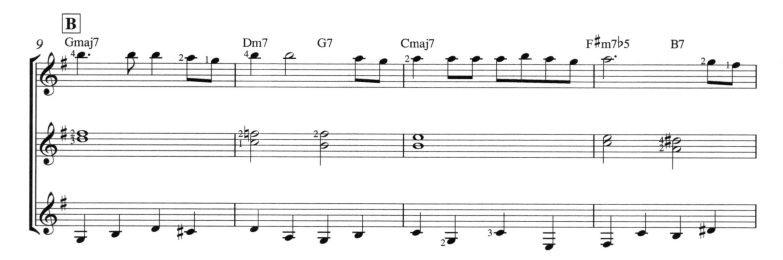

D.S. al Coda

✛ **Coda**

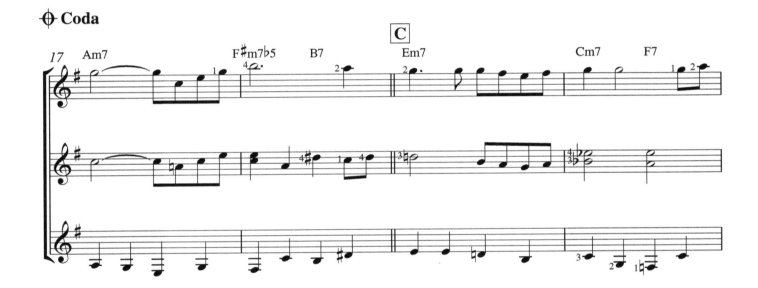

MY FUNNY VALENTINE

from BABES IN ARMS

Words by Lorenz Hart
Music by Richard Rodgers

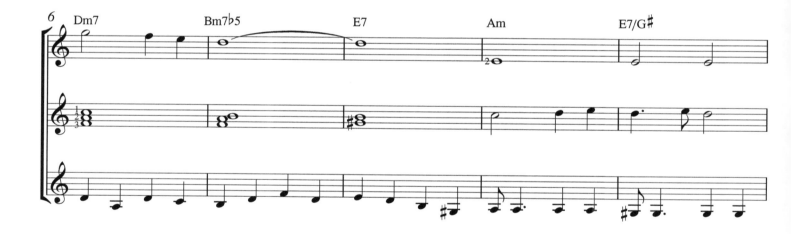

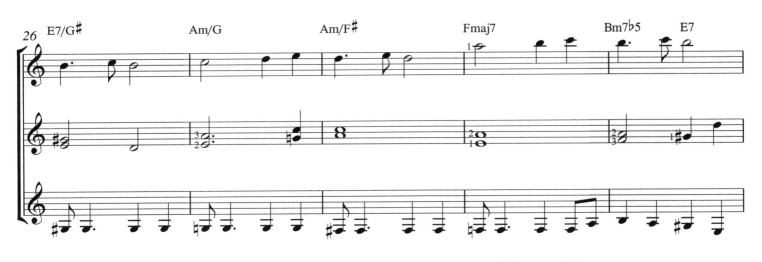

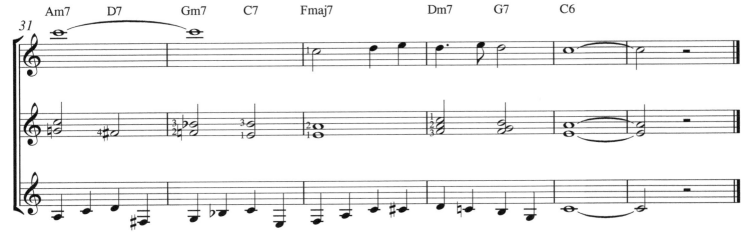

MY ONE AND ONLY LOVE

Words by Robert Mellin
Music by Guy Wood

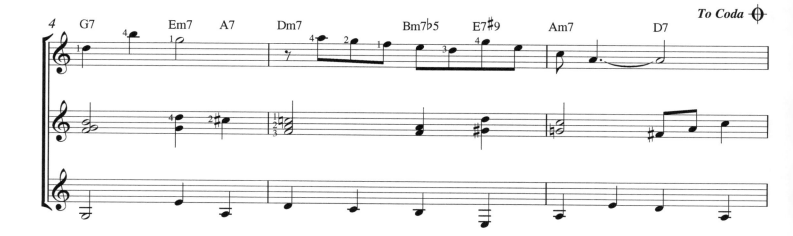

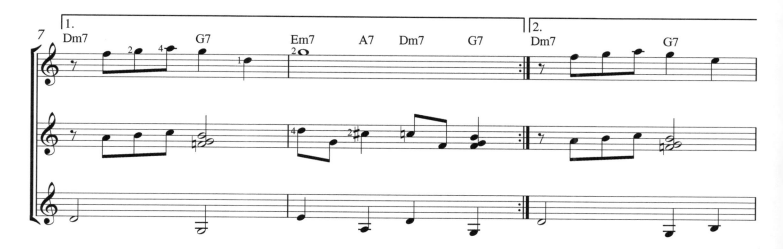

MY ROMANCE

from JUMBO

Words by Lorenz Hart
Music by Richard Rodgers

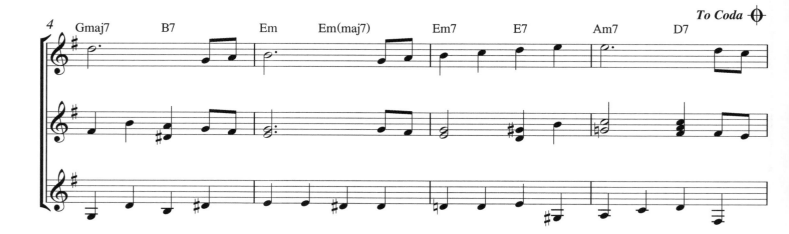

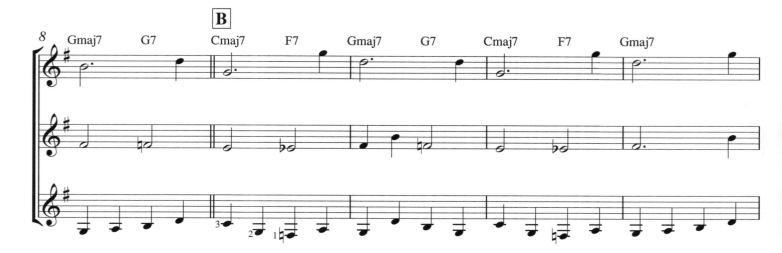

D.S. al Coda

Coda

THE NEARNESS OF YOU

from the Paramount Picture ROMANCE IN THE DARK

Words by Ned Washington
Music by Hoagy Carmichael

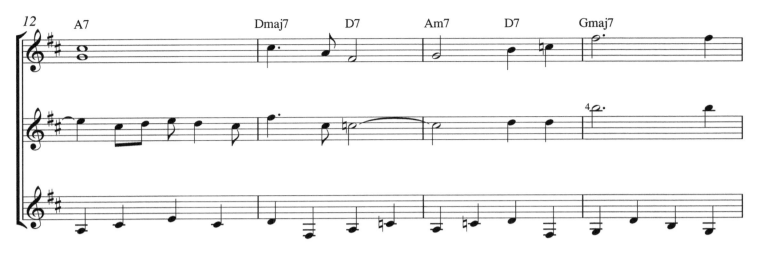

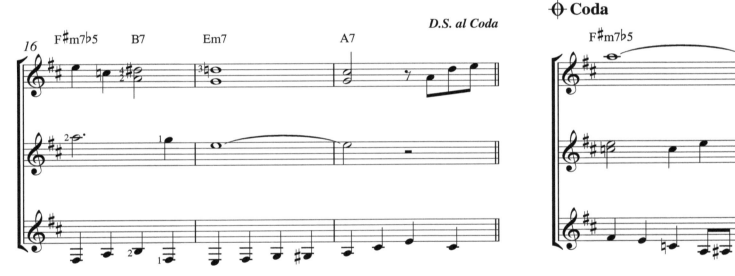

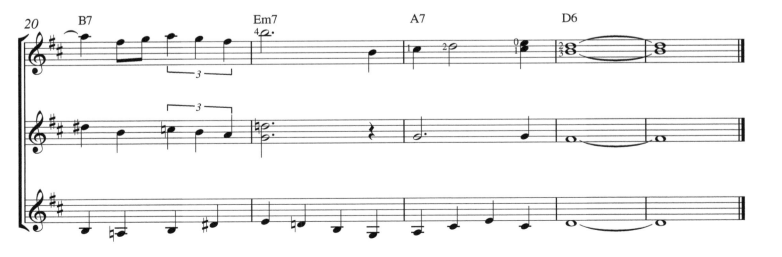

POLKA DOTS AND MOONBEAMS

Words by Johnny Burke
Music by Jimmy Van Heusen

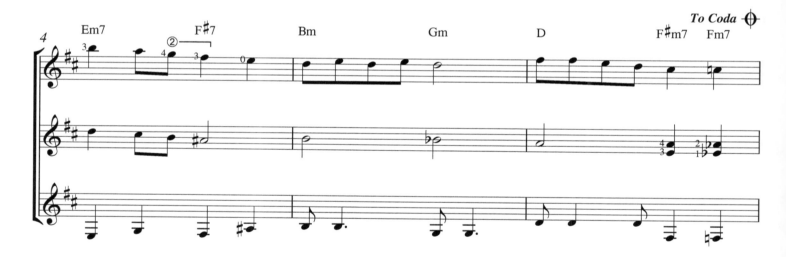

B

D.C. al Coda

Coda

WHEN I FALL IN LOVE

from ONE MINUTE TO ZERO

Words by Edward Heyman
Music by Victor Young

D.C. al Coda

Coda

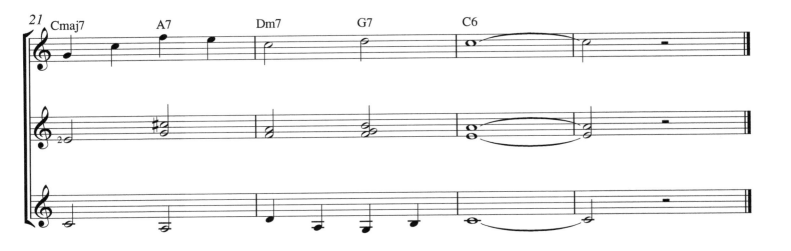

WHEN SUNNY GETS BLUE

Lyric by Jack Segal
Music by Marvin Fisher

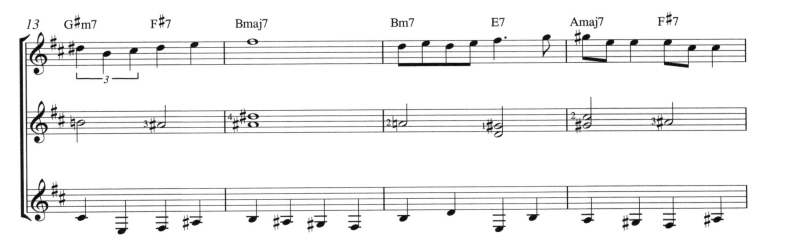

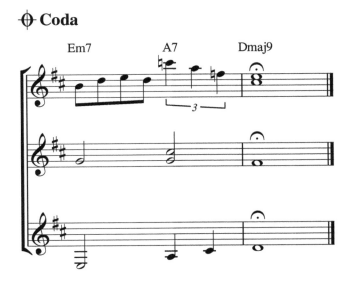

ESSENTIAL ELEMENTS FOR GUITAR

Essential Elements Comprehensive Guitar Method

Take your guitar teaching to a new level! With popular songs in a variety of styles, and quality demonstration and backing tracks on the accompanying online audio, *Essential Elements for Guitar* is a staple of guitar teachers' instruction – and helps beginning guitar students off to a great start. This method was designed to meet the National Standards for Music Education, with features such as cross-curricular activities, quizzes, multicultural songs, basic improvisation and more.

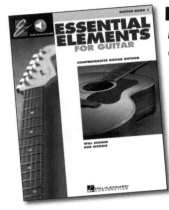

BOOK 1
by Will Schmid and Bob Morris

Concepts covered in Book 1 include: getting started; basic music theory; guitar chords; notes on each string; music history; ensemble playing; performance spotlights; and much more! Songs include: Dust in the Wind • Eleanor Rigby • Every Breath You Take • Hey Jude • Hound Dog • Let It Be • Ode to Joy • Rock Around the Clock • Stand by Me • • Sweet Home Chicago • This Land Is Your Land • You Really Got Me • more!

00862639	Book/Online Audio	$17.99
00001173	Book Only	$10.99

BOOK 2
by Bob Morris

Concepts taught in Book 2 include: playing melodically in positions up the neck; movable chord shapes up the neck; scales and extended chords in different keys; fingerpicking and pick style; improvisation in positions up the neck; and more! Songs include: Auld Lang Syne • Crazy Train • Folsom Prison Blues • La Bamba • Landslide • Nutcracker Suite • Sweet Home Alabama • Your Song • and more.

00865010	Book/Online Audio	$17.9
00120873	Book Only	$10.9

Essential Elements Guitar Ensembles

The songs in the Essential Elements Guitar Ensemble series are playable by three or more guitars. Each arrangement features the melody, a harmony part, and bass line in standard notation along with chord symbols. For groups with more than three or four guitars, the parts can be doubled. This series is perfect for classroom guitar ensembles or other group guitar settings.

Essential Elements Guitar Songs

The books in the Essential Elements Guitar Songs series feature popular songs selected for the practice of specific guitar chord types. Each book includes eight songs and a CD with fantastic sounding play-along tracks. Practice at any tempo with the included Amazing Slow Downer software!

BARRE CHORD ROCK
00001137	Late-Beginner Level	$12.99

POWER CHORD ROCK
00001139	Mid-Beginner Level	$15.99

Mid-Beginner Level
EASY POP SONGS
00865011/$10.99

CHRISTMAS CLASSICS
00865015/$9.99

CHRISTMAS SONGS
00001136/$10.99

Late Beginner Level
CLASSICAL THEMES
00865005/$9.99

POP HITS
00001128/$10.99

ROCK CLASSICS
00865001/$9.99

TURBO ROCK
00001076/$9.95

Early Intermediate Level
J.S. BACH
00123103/$9.99

THE BEATLES
00172237/$9.99

CHRISTMAS FAVORITES
00128600/$9.99

DISNEY SONGS
00865014/$12.99

IRISH JIGS & REELS
00131525/$9.99

JAZZ BALLADS
00865002/$9.99

MULTICULTURAL SONGS
00160142/$9.99

POPULAR SONGS
00241053/$9.99

TOP SONGS 2010-2019
00295218/$9.99

Mid-Intermediate Level
THE BEATLES
00865008/$14.99

BLUES CRUISE
00000470/$9.95

BOSSA NOVA
00865006/$12.99

CHRISTMAS CLASSICS
00865015/$9.99

DUKE ELLINGTON
00865009/$9.99

GREAT THEMES
00865012/$10.99

JIMI HENDRIX
00865013/$9.99

JAZZ STANDARDS
00865007/$12.99

MYSTERIOSO
00000471/$9.95

ROCK HITS
00865017/$9.99

ROCK INSTRUMENTALS
00123102/$9.99

TOP HITS
00130606/$9.99

Late Intermediate to Advanced Level
JAZZ CLASSICS
00865016/$9.99

More Resources

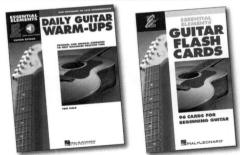

DAILY GUITAR WARM-UPS
by Tom Kolb
Mid-Beginner to Late Intermediate
00865004	Book/Online Audio	$14.99

GUITAR FLASH CARDS
96 Cards for Beginning Guitar
00865000		$10.99

www.halleonard.com

Prices, contents, and availability subject to change without notice.

0621
404